MW00974438

Possessing the Land:

What God Says About

Real Estate

2-21-05

TO Jennifer Ho
Thank You for all your
assistance in the office
We appreciate your help.
May you possess the
territory God has for
you.

By

Edward J. Murray, Jr.

Endorsements

"Possessing Your Land: What God Says About Real Estate provides the knowledge and experience for us to possess our land. Our land is fundamental to possessing our inheritance. Edward Murray has tested and proven the methods outlined in this book in the marketplace and he desires to see the Body of Christ use these methods to advance the kingdom of God."

-Dr. Paul "Buddy" Crum
Sr. Pastor Life Center Ministries

"The prophet Jeremiah said, "Call upon me and I will answer you and show you great and mighty things which you have not known" (Jeremiah 33.3). God is still using His prophets, like Ed Murray, to reveal truth today. Possessing the Land is book that is an outstanding example of this and makes so much sense for the beginning real estate investor because we know from 3 John 2 that God wants His people to prosper."

- Dan Moss
Sr. Vice President-Investments Company

"Edward Murray has some powerful insights and revelation on Possessing the Land. You should buy his book."

- Sheila Zbosnik
Atlanta's TV 57- Producer

Possessing the Land:
What God Says About
Real Estate

All scriptures are quoted from the New International

Version of the Bible.

Published by To His Glory Publishing Company, Inc.

111 Sunnydale Court
Lawrenceville, GA 30044
(770) 458-7947
www.tohisglorypublishing.com

Copyright 2004© Edward J. Murray, Jr. All rights
reserved. No part of this book may be reproduced or
retransmitted in any form or by any means without the
written permission of the author and publisher.

Book is available at:

Amazon.com, BarnesandNoble.com, Borders.com
Booksamillion etc. and other online bookstores.
You can also special order this book through any of your
local bookstores.

Cover Artwork by Suely Sahb
International Standard Book Number: 0-9749802-3-4

Foreword

I am always looking for unique books. *Possessing the
Land: What God says about Real Estate* is an incredible,
unique book for this time. Land has always been such a
prayer focus and issue in my spiritual history. We had
land. We lost land. After marriage, I knew part of my
restoration process would be to buy land again. I also
work very closely with the Host People of North
America, the Native Americans. I have learned so much
about land from them. The Natives have great insight
into the land. That is why I like to read books that
concentrate on the land. Edward Murray has compiled a
book that could be very helpful for Christians to
establish themselves in days ahead. This book will help
you understand the process of land purchase in a
better way.

Psalm 24 says, *"The earth is the Lord's and the fullness
thereof."* So the Lord is always looking for those who
will bring His land into a greater expression of Himself.
In Alistair Petrie's book, *Releasing Heaven on Earth*, he
writes, "Land takes on characteristics based on what we
do on it, both good and bad. Land can be either defiled
or blessed by the people who inhabit it. Throughout
Scripture we find numerous examples of how the
stewards of the day had a distinct effect on their
environment. In Genesis 3:17 we [are informed] that the
ground became cursed because of the fallen stewardship
of Adam and Eve, and verses 18 and 19 describe the
'thorns and thistles' that would now be part of their day-
to-day experience as they worked the land. In Genesis 4,
we have an account of Abel's blood crying out from the

ground following his murder at the hands of his brother, Cain. The ground was describing the nature of the untimely stewardship. Genesis 4:11-12 shows the effect on Cain, who was 'driven from the ground' because of the curse placed on him, and we learn that he would 'be a restless wanderer on the earth. Concerning this passage, [Pastor Bob] Beckett states that: 'To be a vagabond means to be homeless, and it is a curse. Moving from place to place leaves one with a desperate feeling of not belonging. Under such circumstances there can be no chance for a vision or a destiny to take root.' But the ground has been crying out for justice!"[i]

This past year I completed a tour of the 50 states with Apostle Dutch Sheets. We visited each state and declared the redemptive gift of God over every state. We declared the land would prosper. We addressed iniquitous patterns in each state and gathered God's people to worship. When we, as the Body of Christ, gather and worship on the land we see a manifestation of God's justice into the iniquitous patterns on earth. We also see heaven opening and His covenant blessings moving from a heavenly realm into the earth. We see angelic forces coming down to help us bring forth God's plan. Healing the land will be connected with individuals. When we worship, an extension of the kingdom of God in heaven begins to manifest on earth.

This book could not have been better timed. This is an unusual book in that it is filled with needed technical knowledge as well as strategy for God's people to advance. If we have a right attitude toward real estate in the future, we will see ecological and economic health coming forth on the land. Edward's views that he presents here should not be taken as "law" or the only way of doing things, but they are a wonderful guide and model concerning real estate and God's plan in the land. We will also see God's people coming forth with a heart to possess and rather than maintain. We will see our personal, corporate, civil and international security develop in a new ways. This is a timely book for a timely season in the earth. *Possessing the Land* will make the earth "more full" of God's glory.

-Dr. Chuck D. Pierce
President, Glory of Zion International, Inc.
Vice President, Global Harvest Ministries

Dedication

I dedicate this book to the Holy Spirit who inspired me to achieve something I had never done before in my life —that is to write this book!

To my beloved wife; Joyce Murray, who is also my best friend and business partner. You prayed and fasted many times for me while I was writing this book. Your prayers were answered.

To all the sons and daughters of the Most High God who believed what the Lord says about possessing the land. May this book give you revelation and strength to take your promised land.

Table of Contents

Preface

This book was written to help millions of believers to obey what the Lord commanded in **Deut. 1:8 which is, to go and possess the land that He has already given to them.** It is intended to give the reader some understanding about modern day real estate and how it relates to the Word of God. It will help you develop your faith in God in order to get to your "Promised Land" or the territory that God has called you to posses and occupy. This book will also expose the subtle ways of the spirit of Baal and how it operates in the real estate business today. This spirit tries to control, intimidate and manipulate the real estate business world today. This spirit is also known as the spirit of witchcraft. Just like in the past when there was a showdown between the Prophet Elijah and the prophets of Baal, we must confront and defeat this spirit. Nevertheless, God used this man of God (Elijah) that was outnumbered 900 to 1 to bring down the spirit of Baal. The children of Israel chose to watch him instead of being on his side and help him to destroy the prophets of Baal. **As we saw in 1Kings 18:24, only the God who answers by fire was on the side of this one man.** God used him to consume the gods of his time.

Just like today when the odds seem overwhelming and no one is standing with you, our

God who answers by fire, will show up for you today just like He did for the Prophet Elijah. The Word of God says in **James 5:17 that Elijah was a man just like us. He prayed earnestly that it would not rain, and it did not rain for three and half years. Again, he prayed and the heavens gave rain and the earth produced its crops.** You and I have the same power available to us if we believe God in order to get into home ownership, to take new territories, title deeds, to see our cities and surrounding communities transformed and overflowing with every good thing.

This book will help you gain more knowledge in buying a house and going even further into investment properties. I believe this is one area of transformation of wealth that the believer is coming into and it has already started. We must be a part of the tidal wave of transformation of wealth, just as in the book of Acts when believers were homeowners, landowners. They sold off land from time to time in order to bring the proceeds to the apostles and they placed the proceeds at the apostle's feet as we saw demonstrated in **Acts 4:34-35**.

Today, we are to posses our land and effectively occupy the real estate industry so that we have more than enough to give to a local pastor, ministry leader, mission and other organizations so that they can produce fruit in their ministries. You should read this entire chapter in the book of Acts so that you can see the great power of God that was released in the city when they were giving outrageously.

This book will help enable you to go and possess the land or home that God wants to give you because He has promised many times that it is your inheritance from Him. If you read **Isaiah 61:7, God said, instead of shame, my people will receive a double portion and instead of disgrace. They will rejoice in their in heritance; and so they will inherit a double portion in their land**. This is just one scripture that tells us that God will not only give you a double portion in the natural things, but will also give you a double portions in the land in which you are living. Yes, that is real estate! So, begin to shout for those walls of Jericho to come down in your life and march on to your Jordan to possess the land like Joshua did. Every battle was different for him and so will it be for you also! Have faith in God to see the Promised Land that is in store for you.

-Edward J. Murray

Acknowledgements

Special thanks to Suely Sahb, the artist and our good friend from Brazil who was inspired by the Holy Spirit to paint the cover of this book. You are a special blessing to the body of Christ and to us. We love you very much!

Thanks to my family, Ed Murray Sr, Brad, Breezy, Gerry and Von Mann and my Mother in-law, Maria de Jesus. Thank you for all your prayers, encouragement and support.

Ronnie and Wendy Winstead, who helped with the editing and transcribing of this book.
You helped propelled me to get this book done.

Marcus Shirley, a friend who God has chosen to help me learn real estate. You helped instruct and walk me thru some pre-foreclosures and Foreclosures processes. I call you Mr. Foreclosure. Thank you.

All the students who attended our investment classes and who on more than one occasion said that I should write a book. Moses (a student in the class), the Holy Spirit used you to speak the final confirmation to me that it is God's will for me to write a book.

Thank you Prophetess Mary Ogenaarekhua, you helped me with the editing and other work that had to be done in this book. You are a blessing to the body of Christ.

Chapter 1

Possessing the Land

My name is Edward Murray. My wife (Joyce Murray) and I are real estate agents and investors. We are Holy Ghost filled, and would like to talk to you about **Possessing the Land**. God has placed in my heart the desire to help hundreds of thousands of people get into home ownership. My goal is **to see every Christian possess land, houses, apartments buildings, shopping malls and the biggest buildings in the cities.** God has also put in my heart that this is the time and the season for us believers to possess the inheritance He has for us who believe in his son Jesus Christ. The Book of Ecclesiastes says that you should **know the time and the season**.

I believe this is a season of possessing land, possessing houses, possessing territories and possessing the things that God has prepared for us. We have to go and possess the land. We must go in a spirit of faith in order to take the land just like Joshua and Caleb did. Let us take a look at **Deuteronomy 1:8**. The Word says, **"See I have given you the land, go and take possession of the land that the Lord swore He would give to your forefathers, to Abraham, Isaac, Jacob and their descendents after them."** We are the descendents after them. We are the spiritual children of Abraham. We have been grafted into God's family tree through Jesus Christ our Lord.

Our first investment house was a great lesson in how God turns what the enemy meant for evil into good. We took a risk and invested in a house that was four-sided brick, and no garage. It was over 40 years old and had no carpet and no central A/C. It was had three bedrooms and 1.5 baths. The kitchen floor was all torn up, and there were holes in one wall and they were the size of watermelons.

There was even blood on the wall in one of the bedrooms. The previous owner had pulled off the plumbing systems in the bathroom and kitchen. **My wife and I prayed and had faith in God that we could make this house a blessing for someone else.** We bought the house for $78,000. We took about two months to renovate the house. My wife picked out the paint colors, carpet and trim. We had our dear pastor friends (the Sanchez family from Guatemala) pray over the land. They helped us to do a prayer walk of the entire backyard, front yard and inside the house looking for items that did not belong in the house spiritually. We found a silver spoon buried in the backyard. Pastor Cesar told us that witches sometimes put items in people's yards as a curse on their poverty. He had no idea that the previous owner had lost this house due to foreclosure. We also found a half buried brick in the yard with the inscription of the name of a saint on it!

We spent a little more money than we expected to and we used most of the money we had in savings. It was exciting to see what this house that we had totally renovated looked like when it was finished. **We anointed the land with oil, wine and salt. Biblically, the salt represented the healing of the land, the wine represented the blood of Jesus that helps cleanse the sin of the land and the oil represented the anointing.**

Pastor Cesar Sanchez, Joyce and I each poured out these three elements over the four corners of the property. We broke all curses we perceived were on the property in the name of Jesus and we asked God to open the heavens over the house. When we were praying over the land, we had one person; Pastor Cesar represent the blood and my wife represented the salt and I held the oil, which represented the anointing. We poured the elements over the four corners of the property, each one of us holding one element and agreeing together in faith as we prayed.

Land is defined by law as the surface of the earth extending down to the center and upward to the sky, including all natural things thereon such as trees, crops, or water, plus the minerals below the surface and the air rights above. And I thought it was interesting how our courts define land. In **Matthew 16:19,** we see spiritual boundaries even extending to the heavens, **"I will give you the keys of the kingdom of Heaven. Whatever you bind on earth will be bound in Heaven and whatever you loose on earth will be loosed in heaven."** What I believe God is showing us in this scripture is that we have to use our God-given authority on earth as well as in heaven. We must bind and loosen both spiritually and naturally in order to effectively possess our land. If you believe these laws, they will work for you.

Within two weeks we had a buyer for the house. The buyer told me that God was going to do a miracle for her. In my heart, God spoke to me to sell her the house and draw up a contract. The loan office told me not to write up the contract for her because she had bankruptcy on her record from two years before, but God told me to work with her. I am glad I was obedient to listen to the Lord. We ended up closing a little late, but we were all happy at the closing; she and her family had their first house! At closing, the attorney left the room for about twenty minutes. This gave me time to present the Gospel of Jesus Christ and speak some prophetic words to her and her husband. She was impacted by the presence of God and she started to weep. She and her entire family accepted Christ at closing. I told her that the house was a gift from God to her because no one else believed in her but God. The Lord literally helped her to possess the land against all odds.

A couple of months later, my wife and I were directed by the Holy Spirit to go and see how she and her family were doing. She answered the door and was so happy. She told us that her house was the most popular house in the neighborhood. She said that all the children in the neighborhood come outside her house to play. We told her that we had prayed and blessed the land and that we had asked God to make the house a blessing for a family. We had invested $12,000 in the house and made $28,000. That's more than a 200% profit, plus we won an entire family to the Lord. God is so good!

What God did through my wife and I is known as marketplace evangelism; being prepared to present the gospel anywhere, anytime to anyone with boldness and humility. I want to remind you that this was the first investment property we worked on. We had used almost everything we had in our savings to take a leap of faith (investing without looking at the odds) in doing something that we had never done before and God was faithful to come through with His promises. Concerning facing the impossible things of life, Jesus said in **Matthew 19:26, "With man, this is impossible but with God all things are possible."** Therefore, I say to you that God will make the impossible to become possible for you when you trust Him by stepping out in faith.

Chapter 2

Against the Odds

I want to tell you that **Deuteronomy 1:8** said, **"Go and possess the land."** So, there's an active saying that we have to go and the Lord will show us how. First, He showed Moses saying, **"This is the land I'm about to give you."** I believe there are some of you out there that God is showing the land you need to possess. He has already put in your heart the house he wants to give you. And God says to you as you are driving by in your car, **"This is the place I want to give you; this is the duplex I want to give you and this is the apartment building I want to give you. Your land is the house I'm going to give you."** God is nudging you to look at the place. You may have to drive by it as you're going to work or what have you but the bottom line is that you have to be willing to respond to God's gentle tugging in your heart about the land that He has for you.

God asked in **Deuteronomy 3:18, "Have I not given you this land to possess?"** Again, we see in **Deuteronomy 4:22** where He says, **"Now, go over and possess it."** We see a process. The Lord is saying to us, "Son or daughter, I want to give this land or this home to you!" Secondly, He says, "Didn't I tell you to go and take this land?" Now He commands, "Go, go, go!" I want you to get into your heart that this is an on-going process. **We have to stop dreaming, we have to wake up, we have to get into reality and we have to do what it takes to go and possess our land.** I don't want you to miss this next big move of God; **let's ride the tidal wave of transformation of wealth together**. God promised to transfer the wealth of the wicked to the righteous. **Proverbs 13:22**

I want to take you back to Elisha's time as we see here, because this same spirit that operated in Elisha's time is operating in today's world—Baal. Now, the word Baal appears in the Old Testament with a variety of meanings. Sometimes, it is used in the primary sense of master or owner. So you see that the spirit of Baal also means owner! In the Old Testament, we see that Baal represented the idea of one god. In general, Baalam (plural) were the gods of the land, owning and controlling it. The people believed that the increase of crops, fruit and cattle was under the control of these gods. The farmers were completely dependent on the Balaam. The people also believed that some Baals were greater than others and that some were in control of cities. **God has shown me that the spirit of Baal is still at war against the spirit of Elijah today** and we who are believers still wrestle with it today. We see back in that time that there was a struggle between Baalism and Judaism that came to a head on Mt. Carmel. Remember the Prophet Elijah met the 450

priests of Baal and 450 prophets of Asherah and
Elijah put then all to shame. This one man of God
had all of them slain!

We see in **1Kings 18** that Elijah's call to God
was quickly answered and God sent the fire. Jezebel
had the Baalam people there and Elijah said, **"My
God is a God that answers by fire."** We see this
showdown here in **1Kings 18:22** where Elijah said
to them "I am the only one of the Lord's prophets
left but Baal has 450 prophets. Get two bowls for
us, let them choose one for ourselves and let them
cut it into pieces, put it on wood and set it on fire
and I will prepare the other bowl and I will put it on
wood but not set fire to it. Then you call on the
name of your god and I will call on the name of the
Lord. **And the God who answers by fire, he is
God."**

Then all the people said, "What you say is
good." Then Elijah said the to prophets of Baal,

"Choose one of the bowls and prepare it first since there are many of you. Call on the name of your God but do not light the fire." So they took the bowl that was given and prepared it. Then they called on the name of Baal from morning until noon, "Oh Baal, answer us!" They shouted but there was no response. No one answered them and they danced around the altar they had made. At noon, Elijah began to taunt them, "Hey, shout louder! Surely he is a god! Perhaps he is in deep thought or he's busy or he's traveling. Maybe he is sleeping, maybe he must be awakened!" So they shouted louder and they slashed themselves with swords and with spears, as was their custom, until their blood flowed."

This still goes on today in the Middle East where they slash themselves thinking that by cutting themselves, they are inflicting upon themselves the just punishment. They think that when God sees their actions that He is going to reward their demonic actions. They think that God is going to show up for them as they do this. And Elijah says "Hey, Hey! (I'm paraphrasing here) maybe he's in the bathroom, maybe he doesn't hear you, and maybe he's traveling. Maybe he's on vacation, right now." **You see the power and the boldness of Elijah; he's even taunting these 900 prophets. He's outnumbered 900 to 1.** The children of Israel made no decision to stand with Elijah but stayed on the sidelines watching! Which brings us to my next point. Today, most of the church is sitting on the sidelines watching as few of the apostles, prophets, pastors and teachers are engaged in the battle with Baal. We need to jump in and take side with the men and women of God so that we can see our God answer by fire.

Chapter 3

The Battle for Land

There was such boldness on the Prophet Elijah in the Old Testament and now we also have resurrection power and boldness in us. **Acts 4:31 says, "And they were all filled with the Holy Spirit and they spoke the Word of God boldly."** I want to tell you that we need that same kind of boldness to go and to fight the Baal that exists today and that tries to control land and ownership, because you, my beloved, are the true owner. You have all the rights. God has already said, "I've given you this land."

I also want to tell you that **Psalms 37:22** says, **"Those the Lord blesses will inherit the land."** Also **Psalms 37:29** says, **"The righteous shall inherit the land."** It is again stated in **Psalms 135:12, "And He gave their land for a heritage."**

We see here that the Lord has given us an inheritance, both spiritually and naturally. We're still coming head-on with the spirit of Baal and the spirit of Elijah in us must arise.

Let me tell you, I see the spirit of Baal at work all the time in the banking community and in the real estate community. There is so much confusion, there's so much lies, there's so much deception that it makes you want to arise and confront it when you discern it. **The Lord needs Christians like you and I to get in and to take the banking industry.** He needs those of us that will do it right and that will not to lie but are creative in our finances. You can do it because He has promised that to you. There is another promise I want to share with you. I want you to get these promises deep in your heart. Hopefully, my beloved, that will prepare you to go and to take the land, because first you need to get a sense that God wants to bless you with land.

You have to know that it is your rightful inheritance to take land. Right now, we're talking about the old covenant, but you know what? We have a greater covenant in the New Testament and I am going to get into what Jesus said about that too. We are heirs; we are joint heirs and we are the seed of Abraham. **Isaiah 61: 6-7 says, "You will be called priests of the Lord, you will be named ministers of our God. You will feed on the wealth of nations and in their riches, you will boast. Instead of shame, my people will receive a double portion." So they will inherit a double portion in their land.** This is received by faith and action. We need to just walk into it. "Instead of disgrace they will receive their inheritance." So you see that you will inherit a double portion in the land and everlasting joy will be yours. You see, my beloved, it says in Proverbs that when God gives you a gift He will add no trouble to it. Here, we see that not only does He want to give you one piece of land, but He also wants to give you a double portion. That is not just land though but many, many other things.

We see here, that He wants you to rejoice in your inheritance and He wants to give you a double portion in land. So again, we see there is a double portion and I want you to get that into your mind. I want you to get into your heart and your spirit that there is a double portion that you need to receive as a joint heir of God in Christ Jesus. We sit in the heavenly places and the Lord wants you to be blessed now, not when you die. He wants you to be blessed now so you can be a blessing to your children and your children's children. That's why God sets up this wealth and He sets up the land.

We saw in **1Kings 18:29** that, midday passed and the prophets of Baal continued their frantic prophesying even until the time of the evening sacrifice but there was no response, no one answered and no one paid attention. Then Elijah said to the people, 'Come here,' and they came and saw as he repaired the altar of the Lord that was in ruins. Elijah took twelve stones; one for each tribe that descended from Jacob to whom the word of the Lord came, saying "Your name shall be Israel."

With these stones he built an altar in the name of the Lord, dug a trench around it. The trench was large enough to hold two seahs of seed. He arranged the wood, cut the bull to pieces, and laid it on the wood. Then he said to them, 'Fill four large jars of water and pour it on the offering and on the wood. 'Do it again he said.' They did it again. 'Do it a third time he ordered' and they did it a third time. The water ran down around the altar and even filled the trench. At the time of the evening sacrifice, the Prophet Elijah stepped forward and prayed "Oh Lord, God of Abraham, Isaac and Israel, let it be known today, that you are God in Israel and that I am your servant. I have done all these things at your command. Answer me, Oh Lord. **Answer me so these people will know, Oh Lord, that you are God and that you are turning their hearts back again."**

Then the fire of the Lord (Verse 38) fell and burned up the sacrifice, the wood, stones and soil and also licked up the water in the trench. When all people saw this, they fell prostrate and cried "Oh Lord, He is God! Lord, He is God" Then Elijah commanded, "Seize the prophets of Baal, and don't let anyone get away" They seized them and Elijah had them brought down to the Keishon Valley and they were slaughtered there."

Chapter 4

Stepping Out for the Impossible

We see that God used one man. Just one man of God stepped out in faith against 450 prophets of Baal and 450 prophets of Asherah and he had no support from Israel but God used him in spite of lack of support and against all odds.

The Lord sometimes calls us for the impossible and I want to tell you that sometimes it does seem impossible to get land or to even get your first house. I want to tell you today that there is an enemy; Baal that stands in your way. It could be debt, it could be unbelief, it could be doubt, it could even be your mind, it could be no money and it could be a generational curse. These are the giants in your life. That is why I am imparting words of knowledge and wisdom to you and sharing scripture with you. There is nothing like the Word of God!

That is why I say that you have to get these principles into your heart so that you can get creative and know that God has given you an inheritance and a mandate to go and take the land. **Now, we know that land is mentioned over 1400 times in the Bible** so I would say that land therefore is pretty relevant.

The Word of God says in **Philippians 4:13 that "you can do all things through Christ Jesus who strengthens you." Believe therefore that you can do all things.** All means <u>all</u> and that includes land. I want to tell you that this is a scripture that I have meditated on and declared many times in my life and believe in my heart that it is true. In real estate, you truly need the strength of God to accomplish and defeat the powers and principalities that control the land. I also believe worship is a major key in the coming years to see the walls of Jericho come down in people's lives. What an amazing sight it will be, to see the supernatural hand of God smashing the wall that separates you and your inheritance or land!

Chapter 5

The Miracle City – Almolonga, Guatemala

I remember one time we visited in Guatemala, Almolonga Guatemala, a dear friend of ours, Pastor Mariano Riscajche. He went into **2 Chronicles 7:14** and preached on a verse that states, **"If my people who are called by my name will humble themselves, and pray and seek My face and turn from their wicked ways, then I will hear from heaven, and will forgive their sin and heal their land."** There are three things that we need to do: 1) We need to humble ourselves. 2) We need to pray. 3) We need to turn from our wicked attitudes and actions in our hearts. I want to challenge you to ask God to search your heart for the rocks that block your destiny. Ask God to remove those rocks.

I literally saw a city and the land transformed. I just never saw anything like it. I have been to several countries. I have been all over the United States; traveled all over four or five continents but I will tell you, I've never seen anything like Almolonga, Guatemala. It is also mentioned in the transformation video from the Centennial Group. As you walk through Almolonga, there was this electrifying power of that was surging through the atmosphere. It affected even the farm produce in the region. We saw carrots the size of half your arm and cabbages twice the size of a man's head.

Almolonga, Guatemala - population 20,000. Approximately twenty years ago, in Almolonga, they were producing only one truckload of vegetables a week. There was a 92% adult alcoholic rate. They had 36 bars in the city, a divided church, the church buildings were empty and few people were born again. **Today,** there is a 0% alcoholic rate, no bars, no jails, no crime, no poverty and 40 truckloads of exported vegetables per week. There is no idol worship but a united church. There are 20 church buildings full, and 98% "born again" people in the church that are actively serving God. **Literally, there is no poverty and there is no debt. They have eradicated poverty from this city! All of this started with one pastor and five intercessors.** The Bible says in **Ezekiel 22:30, "So I sought for a man among them who would make a wall and stand in the gap before me, on behalf of the land, that I should not destroy it, but I found no one."**

In Almolonga, everyone pays cash for everything including vehicles like Mercedes Benz! We learned that the reason the people like to buy Mercedes Benz was because it is well built and very durable. They need something that is going to last a long time. They also import lots of other types of vehicles from Europe.

We saw that in Almolonga, the people would literally pray over the land in obedience to **2 Chronicles 7:14** that says, **"If my people who are called by my name will humble themselves and pray and seek My face, and turn from their wicked ways, then I will hear from heaven, and will forgive their sin and heal their land."** These people bless the land and they ask God to heal the land as they pray.

This is something we need to do also in the United States; it's just a great example of how God can heal the land and cause the transformation of an entire city. It is well known that Pastor Mariano has seen over 30 people resurrected from the dead. I asked Pastor Mariano, "How do you pray for somebody that is dead?" To me that is a legitimate question. He said, **"You don't just pray, but you**

just believe that it's going to be done! You can't have doubt and unbelief; you just believe." Many miracles were done through his wife also. We heard reports that his wife would sometimes hold in her arms, babies with skulls that were crushed in due to different incidents and accidents and God would heal them. The skulls would pop back out! Wouldn't it increase your faith if you saw something like that?

They saw so many blessings and healings because they were after the well being of the land, they were after the well being of the community and they were after the transformation of their city. As we were traveling to Almolonga, we accidentally took a wrong turn in the road and ended in a different city. In contrast to Almolonga, you could sense poverty, alcoholism, depression and the spirit of witchcraft. The driver was told us we were only ten miles from Almolonga but I didn't believe it. This city that was only ten miles away from

Almolonga was still held bound by Satan and his demons. At first, I thought that it was Almolonga but in my spirit, I knew that this was not the miracle city that we heard about. I was so relieved when we finally got to Almolonga and especially when I saw the great contrast between the two cities. Why was this other city a stronghold of Satan and Almolonga had been transformed? I believe one of the reasons is because the people in Almolonga prayed and fasted at least three days a week for their community. **Mark 9:29** This kind can come out by nothing but prayer and fasting. The pastors of the different denominations meet at least once a month to keep communication open and to keep out the spirit of suspicion among them.

My beloved, that is where we need to get it; not just in church but we need to go out into the community and see transformation. I am telling you that have seen it firsthand in Almolonga. This is why Almolonga is called the Miracle City.

Almolonga is just amazing! We brought Pastor Mariano to Atlanta a couple of years ago and we had some meetings here for transformation of the city. Recently, I talked to one of the pastors who had Pastor Mariano minister in their church. He told me that their church has never been the same since Pastor Mariano prayed corporately against the principalities in the region. It has grown spiritually and he wants me to bring him back again. Let me tell you, it is such a powerful corporate anointing to bring down city strongholds on this man that I have not seen on too many men of God, but he is very humble. Inspite of all his achievements, he will take the time to sit and talk with you. **2 Corinthians 10:4 "For the weapons of our warfare are not carnal but mighty in pulling down strongholds."**

One of the reasons the people fasted and prayed three times a week was because they needed to drive out the spirit of Mashimo—the principality that they believe smokes cigars, drinks alcohol and chews tobacco! To us, this is a most ridiculous belief but the native people in Almolonga believe that this spirit is real. This principality even has spiritualists that serve it. As they worship, they would sometimes go through the town with their incense and the people would bring alcohol, tobacco and cigars to honor this principality! At one time, the jails were full of alcoholics because this principality promotes lewdness and alcoholism.

Pastor Mariano and his wife fasted and prayed and asked God to drive out the principality and God did after years of their intense prayers. **Now the town is 99% Christian, debt-free, no poverty and the jails are shut down and the sheriff has no work.** Would it not be nice to have this happen in our cities! They drove the evil spirits out! They chased them out! Furthermore, they took possession of their land and believed in the inheritance that God had promised them in **Isaiah 61:7.**

Ephesians 6:12:

> **"For our struggle is not against flesh and blood, but against the rulers, against the authorities, against the powers of this dark world and against spiritual forces of evil in heavenly realms."**

Now, I want to tell you something and that is, that the word **"possession"** in Hebrew is **"yarosh."** It means, **"to occupy by driving out previous tenants"** and possessing it. We have to drive out the previous tenants and possess our land. Now this can happen through a process called foreclosure or like a "fixer-upper" or like an estate that needs to be sold. Who knows what situation you have to drive out? Whatever the situation is, you must be willing to drive out those things that seek to prevent you from possessing your land. You have to seize your inheritance and cast out or dispose of all opposing forces. You may have to pray and fast in order to posses the land that God has for you and your family.

Chapter 6

God is the Owner, We are the Stewards

Beloved, we have to set our hearts right. **Why is God going to give us wealth?** I want to take you to **Acts 4:32**. There is a correlation with wealth here and the Lord showed me the scripture. I just kept meditating on it and I kept going back to it until I got the full revelation of what the Lord showed me. Actually, there is a lot here but let me outline it for you. It says, in **Acts 4:34, "There were no needy persons among them. From time to time those who owned land or houses sold them and they brought the money from the sales and put it at the apostles' feet and it was distributed to anyone had a need."**

Wouldn't that be awesome? Not only do you have a home but also you see here that some of these disciples were landowners and homeowners. They owned lands and houses and I believe that some of them owned more than one house or one piece of land. This is another reason why God wants you to have a double portion in the land you live in. God gave them these lands because they were **good stewards and they had a heart to give when the kingdom of God needed finances.**

First of all, we have to understand that we are stewards; we are not really the rightful owners. This is an inheritance that God gives us and wants to release to us when we have the right attitude in our hearts. **James 1:17** states that, **"Every good and perfect gift comes down from the Heavenly Light who does not change like shifting shadows."** He does not change, "He is the same yesterday, today and forever."

We see here that these were landowners and that they would sell off to give to the church or to the kingdom of God. That is why God is going to set you up. If you go at it saying, "Lord, I would love to give a million dollars, I would love to give houses away." God is going to see to it that you get it. We have to prepare our hearts just like the saints that we read about in the Book of Acts. If we go back to **Acts 4:32**, we will see that it says, **"All the believers were one in heart, in mind and no one claimed that any of his possessions were his own but they shared everything they had. With great power the apostles continued to testify of the resurrection of the Lord Jesus and much grace was upon them all."** I believe that as we begin to increase in our giving to the church, we will see an explosion of God's power being released through acts of kindness. The church needs to be more humble and less controlling. It should let people go for the territories that God has given them without being insecure. We all need to truly believe that promotion comes from the Lord and that nobody can steal our destiny.

Chapter 7

One Heart, One Mind, One Spirit:

Marching to the Same Beat

Beloved, we have to get together as a corporate church and not just as one church but as in plural churches. **We have to get one heart and one mind.** And we have to get into a mindset that we are all together. We may disagree on some things but let us put those aside and let us be like the example in the book of Acts where most of the miracles occurred outside the walls of the church. Can you imagine if somebody sees someone move in great power, or if somebody gets healed? I guarantee you in the name of Jesus that many people are going to get saved from that.

Here there is a correlation; they were of one heart and one mind. **They did not claim any of their possessions were their own.** That is the key; that God is the owner, we are just stewards over what He gives us. You know if **He can trust you with little, He can trust you with much.** He is going to start you with little. He is going to see how much He can trust you with then as you are a good steward, He will give you more and more. Those who are not good stewards of what He has given them, even the little that they have, scripture says, shall be taken away from them. He will give it to someone else who is a good steward over it as Jesus stated in **Luke 19:26**.

My wife and I always pray that the Lord would make us good stewards. My heart's cry is, "Lord, I want to be a landowner and I want to be a homeowner. I want to be renting homes to pastors and missionaries. I want to bless them." God answered the cry of my heart. Do you know that now we have houses that we sometimes rent to God's ministers? We always put them in our houses because we want to be a blessing to them. They take care of the house and we just charge them what the mortgage would normally be. We do not try to make money off of them but they have a nice house that is better than an apartment. Most real estate investors will not do this. Every situation is different. So you need to inquire of God as to what to do.

I tell people, if you are in an apartment you will be fortunate if you got your deposit back when you move out but when you sell a house you can make thousands of dollars. When you see your house as an investment and not just a place to live, you will do everything in your power to take care of it and the value of the house can appreciate. Since the mortgage rates have been at an all time 40-year low and there are all kinds of loan programs out there to help you, I do not want to hear excuses about why you are not planning to buy a house.

I have watched the internationals (foreigners) that live in this country. I have noticed how they work with other family members to help support their families financially and emotionally. They help each other by co-signing to buy houses. They would partner with someone (usually a relative or a friend) with good credit in their effort to help each other get into a house. They stick together and they go out and they possess land. They are buying up the houses. Beloved, you can do the same so just ask God whom to pair with. If you have no credit, you know that there are all kinds of good creative financing out there. What I am seeing here is how the foreigners in America will help other family members to obtain or to possess a house for a family member. They also have a lot of faith to go after a lot of land and territory.

Chapter 8

A New Revelation for Your Home

We actually saw the healing of the land in Guatemala and it just transformed my mind. When you see something of God in action, it is like a fresh revelation in your spirit, and your spirit man says, **"We can do this in the United States." My question is, "Why aren't we doing this?"** We have to become one in unity and in one heart and one mind. I want to read you something that even the secular world is hinting on; they're picking up on this. Beloved, we have to be as wise as a serpent and as gentle as a dove. **We need to understand the times and the seasons we are living in.**

This is from a special report on real estate that was written in 2004 by a major financial magazine. In this 2004 issue it says, **"Your Best**

Investment, Can Real Estate Really Make You Rich?" The editor states that she knows the promise, "the pearl" of owning real estate. It says that all over America, homeowners are gloating over their wealth-building prowess. Thanks to a steady rise in residential real estate prices, the net worth of the American family has reclaimed its Internet bubble heights. Who needs a stockbroker? When a simple three bedroom colonial can double in value in a few years. Who needs to put away cash for retirement when that money in a new bathroom or porch delivers instant asset appreciation? **Real estate is the surest, safest path to wealth and has been since before most of us heard of dot.coms, IPO's and 401-K's.**

The report goes on to say that a home is a special thing; a major investment that the government subsidizes through mortgages, tax break deductions and the only one in which you can take tax free capital gains, plus you get to live in it.

It is a benefit that no stock or fund can provide. This makes your home your most complicated, your most personal, your most emotional and your significant investment. This magazine highlighted lots of things about houses, investing, mortgages and most of the things that you need to know about investing in a home. It was pretty thorough. But, you see, even the secular magazine is picking up on the value of home ownership and what we need to know.

Beloved, it is our time to possess our land. My point is this, if the secular community is getting a revelation, why aren't we? That's why I'm writing this book, to help inspire you to be landowners and homeowners.

Chapter 9

Our Inheritance

Hosea 4:6 says, "My people are destroyed for lack of knowledge." **This is why we need to study and know everything about land and homeownership.** We must also be careful of people that want to take advantage of our lack of knowledge in real estate. A lot of people are taken advantage of by ungodly realtors when they perceive that these people are without knowledge in real estate. This is sad but true, we see this a lot in our profession. So, I encourage you to educate yourself and study about real estate because this will make you more knowledgeable. I want you to know that if you don't have a home you need to get your first house. **You need to "go for it." Again, my question to you is, if not you, who?** And if not now, when? There is such a spirit of procrastination, there is a spirit of doubt and unbelief in America that we need to just get full of faith and rise up as spiritual sons of God and know that the Lord has called us to inherit this land.

I want to tell you something; there are many promises of God in the Bible that we believers can take hold of today. I want you to know that the descendants of Abraham are no longer just the physical nation of Israel but rather the true children of Abraham are those who have faith. **(Galatians 3:7).** **Also Galatians 3:14 says, "Christ died on the cross so that God's blessing, promised to Abraham, might come through Jesus Christ to those who are not Jews!"**

So we see the Lord has engrafted us into the promise. We see that we have a greater covenant— we have a New Testament. In the Old Testament, He promised the land to Abraham and his seed. In the New Testament, we have a greater and deeper covenant, which is Jesus Christ—the seed to which the promise rightly belongs! Therefore, in Christ Jesus, we are the spiritual heirs of Abraham. God promised Abraham the land and He told Abraham that in him would the blessing come upon all nations. In Christ Jesus, we have been called to inherit those promises.

Chapter 10

The Process for Getting Your Land

The following chapters in this book will explain a little bit of the process in getting a home. It will give you some understanding of the basic process of getting a home.

I want to tell you here about getting your first home. Before you located a home of your liking or choice, you need to do the following.

1. **You need to hire a home inspector** (that costs between $200 and $300). The home inspector will take pictures of the house. The inspector will inspect the house for you and look for any problems.

2. **You can also buy a home warranty for generally around $360 to $400.** It will

71

cover your plumbing, your electrical, your appliances, your heater, your air conditioning unit, your septic etc. You have to read through the policies but generally it covers the most major things in a house.

3. You need to find a good realtor. This is important because they pull a CMA (a Comparable Market Analysis) for you. They will not do an appraisal but they will do a CMA and generally they pull three comparable properties sold in the neighborhood. Your first time of buying a home, you should have a realtor just to help you so that you do not pay too much for a house. You do not want to buy an overpriced house. We have seen many times how people are taken advantage of. They do not get a realtor because think they know the market and they go out and buy a house. If they need to sell it in a year or two, then they run into trouble because they paid too much and they have no equity on the house. They then have to pay commissions out of their pocket to the real estate agents in order to sell their house.

This situation, where you have to pay out of your pocket to sell the house is what is called, in real estate, **"upside-down transaction."** This means the homeowner will pay more out of pocket to close the transaction. **A good realtor will keep you from this by making sure that you do not overpay for a house.** You can e-mail us at or call us at ejmenterprise@bellsouth.net and we can refer you to an agent in your area.

4. Another important aspect is location. You need to find out where you want to live or where you want to be. This is very important. Do you want to be close to work or do you want to be in the country or you do you want a shorter commute? You have to decide what neighborhoods, schools systems and all that. You can log on to **Realtor.com** so that you can check all these out.

Also, get a handy man, if you are going to do "fixer-uppers." Find someone in your church who can fix houses. When you choose to buy a "fixer-upper," at first, most of the problems may look devastating or overwhelming but know that that might not really be the case. A lot of it may be cosmetic. I will give you an insider's tip; the most expense in fixing a house is really the flooring, and painting, HVAC system (this is your heating and air conditioning system).

Chapter 11

Investment Properties: This is Where the Money is Made in Real Estate

I want to talk to you about investment properties. **This is another big area I feel that we need to take advantage of as Christians.** I always pray for the **"wealth of the wicked that is stored up for the righteous of Christ" (Proverbs 13:22).** The wicked lay up wealth for the righteous to inherit. That is you and I, beloved.

On investment property, again, my wife and I are real estate agents and investors and we also network with a group of investors and investment companies. We are always looking for deals. We also work with foreclosure agents in Atlanta. A couple of them are some of the biggest in Atlanta, and we do get referrals from them. We know what is on the market; what is "hot," what is ready to sell and we can search that for you very quickly within an hour.

Foreclosure is at an all time high in America and what I think here is that in some cases, people just get over their budget and they pay too much for the house. Normally, it is because of divorce, loss of job or company relocation. A good realtor can help you locate these foreclosed properties.

REO means "real estate owned" properties. They can be fixer-uppers or foreclosures that are due to divorce, lost of spouse, lost of income. There are all kinds of situations that might lead to a foreclosure on a house but as realtors, we get paid to solve problems (i.e., bring buyers and sellers together). When solve a problem, we may become the buyer of the house if there are no buyers and we see that the house has great potentials. We would then take our time to find another buyer for it or we may buy it and rent it out. **You can buy <u>fix and sell</u> or you can buy <u>fix and lease.</u>** You can go to the local government they have programs that pay for single parents to lease a housing from a homeowner.

Some counties have different prices that they will pay the homeowner to rent to the county approved person in county program. When you rent your house to these type of people, you are basically renting to the county government. The government pays the rent directly on a monthly basis into your bank account. Because certain counties have different headquarters, when you decide to rent to county program recipients, know that it is very simple to get on their list to advertise your house. You can also do a lease purchase where you get a down payment for the house and you charge a higher rent for the house and you can generally close on the house in one year. This is called **"a lease purchase."** The advantage of doing "a lease purchase" is that if the purchasers do not close on the house, you normally will keep their down payment and sell the house again to another purchaser. I have known some investors to sell a house four times over. They kept the non-refundable deposit every time until the person buying the home finally closed on the house.

Chapter 12

Taking Out Your Goliath

I want to take you to one scripture here, **Hebrews 9:15, "For this reason, Christ is the mediator of the new covenant, that those who are called may receive the promised eternal inheritance."** Now that He has died as a ransom to set us free from sins committed under the first covenant, beloved, we have a spiritual and natural covenant. We have a better covenant with Jesus Christ! Now, I want to tell you that we need to possess the land. **Philippians 4:13 says, "I can do all things through Christ who strengthens me."** All means all, so I want to encourage you that you can go out and you can do this and get knowledge on this.

We do have C.D.'s and manuals and a web page (<u>www.ufindahouse.com</u>) that can help

you search for foreclosures and "fixer-uppers"
so that you have the knowledge about what you are
doing. You feel more confident and secure to go
out and slay that spirit of doubt and unbelief just
like David took out Goliath with one stone. The
bigger the challenge, the bigger your reward will be.
It takes faith to confront your Goliath but without
faith, we cannot please God **(Hebrews 11:6,).**
"And without faith it is impossible to please God,
because anyone who comes to Him must believe
that He exists and that He rewards those who
earnestly seek Him." Here God says that not only
do you need faith, you also have to earnestly seek
Him and there is a reward for those who do.

Know that in a lot of things, the bigger the
risk, the bigger the reward. Always remember that
the bigger the giant, the bigger the reward, so we
can be like David. David did not call right away for
the intercessors. David did not call for a meeting.
David did not call for new anointing. David just

went. Instead of thinking and taking time to see if it was God's will, he just went out and grabbed those five (5) smooth stones. He grabbed more than one because he was not only going to take out Goliath but he was ready to take out his other brothers if they came after him too. David might have been thinking, "Man, this Goliath is such a big target, how could anybody miss him?"

I want to encourage you, just begin to grab your rock in the spirit and go after that spirit of Baal or that spirit of Goliath that is taunting you. Grasp hold of faith in Jesus and become the warrior that God sees you as and go destroy that spirit of doubt, unbelief, poverty and mocking. Get away from people who speak doubt and unbelief and get around people who are of like mind as you; people who are full of the spirit of faith. You have to do this in order to keep your faith at the level that you can receive from God. Get around people who are already anointed to posses the land and it will help propel you to your next level. The experience of slaying your Goliath will help you walk into your promised land.

I want to tell you that this investment property idea in real estate is a big deal. We need to own **not just one home but an investment home as well.** Remember that promise in **Isaiah 61:7 that we would inherit a double portion in this land.** We need to go after that double portion in our lives.

Chapter 13

ROI:

A Good Return on Your Investment

I want to encourage you to start praying, fasting and seeking God on this issue of possessing the land. Again, my question is why not you and if not you, who? I believe that God has called us to help you. Just a reminder, that we have professionally edited tapes and C.D. with a manual that is titled, *"The Basic Nuts and Bolts for Real Estate Investors."* You can e-mail us at *ejmenterprise@bellsouth.net.* The C.D. series is a one-day seminar edited on tape or C.D. This is loaded with a wealth of information that can save you thousands of dollars.

I want to tell you that God expects a return on His investment. You may be saying, "Where is that in scripture?" I will tell you, it is in **Luke 19:11**. This is the parable of the ten minas. This is where the manager gave one servant one mina (money) and another servant another mina. He gave three people money to invest, two of the three made the money by investing and the manager said, "Because you have been trustworthy in a small matter, take charge of ten cities." The other servant he told to take charge of five cities. The third servant said, **(Luke 19:20)** "See sir, here is your mina, I have kept it laid away in a piece of cloth. I was afraid of you, because you are a hard man. You take out what you did not put in and reap what you did not sow."

His master replied, "I will judge you by your own words. You wicked servant! You knew that I am a hard man; taking out what I did not put in and reaping what I did not sow?

Then why did you not put my money on deposit, so that when I came back, I could have collected it with interest?" Then he said to those standing by, "Take the mina away from him and give it to the one who has ten minas." When those He spoke to told him that the first servant already has ten minas, He replied, "I tell you that to everyone who has, more will be given, and as for the one who has nothing, even what he has will be taken away."

We see here that Jesus is telling the story and that God is the investor, our manager. He expects a return on His investment. This is not only money, but also talents that God has given you and Jesus gave us a revelation in this scripture. He wants you to use your talents and gifts wisely or else they will be taken away from you when God judges your stewardship. We see here in Verse 22 that **He called the servant who hid his money a "wicked servant."** In other words, Jesus is rebuking this servant for not investing at all. **He**

did not even put the money in the bank to at least earn interest.

I want to challenge you to ask God, "What are my gifts and talents so that I can use them to earn interest for the kingdom of God?" We also see here that there is a connection that Jesus is making between managing money and governing cities. How well you manage money or talent will determine how many cities you will govern. Think about this.

We have had several testimonies where we were able to help people locate properties with a lot of equity, normally at least 20% or more. One 21 year-old investor, who had taken one of our investment classes has already closed on a home. We helped him to make an offer and he got the house for $65,000 but it is worth $114,000! The comparable properties in the neighborhood and subdivision sold for around $114,00.00 and the house is in "country club." Now, let me tell you, at first, he had an agent who would not put an offer for $65,000 on his behalf. I told him, "You can put an offer for any amount that you want. You will not be ashamed because this is a business matter. Don't listen to a real estate agent that doesn't want to write the offers the way you want. Find another agent that will work with you, they're out there." **This young man has over $49,000 plus equity in this house.** Not bad for somebody who had hardly any money in his savings account.

As I said earlier in the book, I call this putting faith in action. Let me tell you, my beloved, this young man is going to move into that house and get a roommate. He had put 10% down and now has enough equity so he will not have to pay primary mortgage insurance. Mortgage insurance alone could add an extra $100 to $150 dollars to person's monthly house payment but this young man will be able to rent out half the house for what he is going to pay for the mortgage. Are you with me? He will not even be paying the mortgage; he has someone else (his roommate) paying for his investment! He will only be paying for electricity, water and gas but someone else will pay for his mortgage. He can live in it for a year or two and sell it and do what is called a **"cash out."** He can also get it refinanced after he fixes it up to get everything in order. He can get 80% or 90% **"loan to value ratio"** loan on that property and pull the difference out on what the pay-off is and on what the new loan amount is. He will get that in cash! Or he can get a home equity loan, which is a big thing right now. **And by the way, this is a loan that is not taxed like earned income.**

In a home equity loan, you **can pull cash out from the equity in your house and it is tax deductible.** You can pay off cars, you can buy whatever you want, and you can take it and buy another investment house. You can use it to get started on fixing up your business property to lease. What a great thing to lease to pastors and to missionaries and to write a good lease agreement. We have several testimonies of people that we find properties for that just never knew anything about it. They attend our class and the next week after the class, they go out looking for properties. They are finding the properties because they are full of faith. They believe the promises of God.

Some of these people are not Christians that walk in faith like the Roman Centurion. Jesus marveled at this Centurion's understanding of authority and faith. He was not of the tribes of Israel. God is so awesome. I remember one time, a gentleman, who is a confessed atheist, took my class on Investment Properties. (I had presented the Gospel to him and he was taking time to make a decision about Christ.) The next week we were looking for a property for him to buy. We found it that same week. It took him over a month to renovate the property. Which, by the way, has 30% equity and he decided to renovate the house and put it up for sale. That is faith in action, by a secular person. He is just about finished with it and should put it on the market soon. These guys are coming in, getting the knowledge, going out and possessing the land. **These are people who normally have never done anything in real estate investment properties before.**

Chapter 14

Having Equity in Your Home:

A New Home Versus a Re-Sale Home

For some reason every first time buyer would like to buy a new home, meaning New Construction. It looks nice, feels nice and you are the first in the home. **The only problem is, there is no deal for the buyer and no equity.** You pay the price the builder wants or go somewhere else and buy a house.

On a re-sale house you can negotiate everything, like closing costs, purchase price, or personal items in the house. This is an excellent opportunity to get equity in a home. I believe in equity because it is like having a savings account. In fact, you can get a home equity loan, which is tax deductible and use it to pay off debt that is not tax deductible, like your car payment, credit cards, student loans, etc. This is using your talents wisely.

I want to add that just because a house is a foreclosure does not mean that it is "fallen down" or in terrible shape. In fact, **we live in a foreclosed house** that just needed cosmetic work like paint and "touch up." It now looks like a new house and already has thousands of dollars in equity.

Buying a new Construction home is nice, but if you get into financial trouble, you have no equity in your house for about 1–2 years and you will not be able to pay commission to agents to help sell your house. If you have equity in your house, you can get a loan that is tax deductible at a low interest rate and get some extra cash to help you through a tight time or to pay off some debt. **It is better if you look at your house like an investment, and one of the biggest you will make in your lifetime.**

Having ownership makes such a big difference as opposed to renting and making someone else rich. At first, owning a home seems like a big responsibility which it is, but like anything else in life, once you have mastered it, you will wish you had bought a home a lot sooner than you did.

I highly recommend that if you are buying a home the first time or the twentieth time that you get a home inspection by a Qualified State Home Inspector. Most real estate agents can recommend 2 or 3 that they know of.

The Home Inspector will probably charge anywhere from $200 to $300. This is a small price to pay for a hundred thousand plus dollar investment. The inspector will check the safety of the house, electrical, plumbing, leaks, appliances, HVAC, foundation, leaks, etc. They will put together in writing, a report on the house. Some good inspectors will take pictures of problem areas so you can understand where and what they have found. This will also give you an idea about what it might cost to repair a "fixer upper," a foreclosure or an investment property.

Chapter 15

Understanding the Different Types of Loan Programs

I want you to shop around for the best rates possible, do no t just go to one loan officer and stick with that officer. Shop around for the best rate you can get and for the lowest origination fee. (This is a fee the loan officer charges for originating the loan; typically it is 1% of the loan amount.) Ask the loan officer for a good faith estimate. This will have a list of what you are being charged for in the loan. It will have estimated taxes, insurance, attorney fees, etc.

A day before closing or 24 hours before closing on a home, ask the attorney to fax or send you a **HUD-1 statement**. This should reflect what you have agreed upon with the loan officer on the good faith estimate. Do not be intimidated about signing all those papers (Loan Application). If something doesn't work out, just walk away. They will not force you to close with that mortgage company. You may lose your appraisal money (approximately $325.00 to $375.00) or credit report ($50.00). This is why I recommend that you shop around so you do not waste your time and theirs.

Conventional Loans are most common in the real estate market. The security for the loan is provided solely by the mortgage; the payment of the debt rests on the ability of the borrower to pay. In making such a loan, the lender relies primarily on its appraisal of security, the real estate. No additional insurance or guarantee on the loan is necessary to protect the lender's interest. You can now get 100% LTV (Loan to Value) Conventional Loans. This means that you do not have to put a down payment on a house. Conventional loans are the most popular and easiest to qualify for. Lenders can set criteria to which a borrower and the collateral are evaluated to qualify for the loan.

You can also qualify for what is called, "stated income programs." This is if you do not show enough money earned on your W-2's or documented income. Another way you can qualify for this is showing three months bank statements and verification of employment. This is an easier way to qualify for a home loan if you did not earn enough income on your W-2's. If your credit score is high enough, there are loan programs called **"No Docs."** This means that no documents are needed for the loan but a 5% down payment, depending on how high your credit score is. This will help you get into a larger house if you do not make enough income.

Chapter 16

Private Mortgage Insurance (PMI)

This insurance protects the lender against the borrower if they default on the loan. One way a borrower can obtain a mortgage loan with lower down payment is under a private mortgage insurance (PMI) program. Because loan-to-value ratio is higher than for other conventional loans, the lender requires additional security to minimize the risk. PMI protects a certain percentage of a loan, usually 25 to 30 percent against borrower default. The borrower pays a monthly fee while the insurance is in force. The premium may be financed. Because only a portion of the loan is insured, once the loan is repaid to a certain lender, the lender may agree to terminate the coverage.

Effective in July 1999, a federal law required that PMI automatically terminate if a borrower,

> 1) Accumulated at least 22% equity in the home.
>
> 2) Is current on Mortgage payments.

Lenders are required by law to inform borrowers of their right to cancel PMI.

The extra PMI payment can add on hundreds of dollars or more a month to your house payment. This is why it is important to try not to pay PMI. I have found that you could pay a higher interest rate and not have PMI and you would still have a lesser house payment.

There is another popular home mortgage, called an 80/20 loan, in which you do not pay the PMI. Let me explain how that is possible if you do not put 20% down payment. You get an 80% first loan and a 20% equity line. The first mortgage is financed at 80% and the second mortgage is financed at 20%. This is typically a higher rate but still a lower monthly payment, if you had to pay PMI.

Chapter 17

FHA and VA Loans

FHA loans are common today. Most people think FHA is a government loan but that is not true. FHA is the abbreviation for the Federal Housing Authority, which operates under HUD. It neither builds homes nor lends money itself. **An FHA loan refers to a loan that is insured by the agency.** These loans must be made by FHA approved lending institutions. **The FHA insurance provides security to the lender in addition to the real estate.** As with private mortgage insurance, the FHA insures lenders against loss from borrower default on a loan. FHA loans are insured by the government, in case the borrowers defaults on a loan. Again, they do not loan money or build houses.

FHA Loans. The most popular FHA program is the Title II, Section 203 (b) fixed rate interest loan. This is for 10 to 30 years on one to four family residences. The borrower is charged a percentage of the loan as a premium for the FHA insurance. The upfront premium is paid at closing by the borrower or some other party. It may be financed along with the total loan amount. A monthly premium also may be charged. The mortgaged real estate must be appraised by an approved FHA appraiser. The loan amount cannot be more than $227,905.00 for a single-family house in the Atlanta area. You can also purchase multiple unit properties with FHA. You can pay off an FHA loan and apply for another one.

VA Loans

VA Loans. The Department of Veterans Affairs commonly known as the VA, is authorized to guarantee loans to purchase or construct homes for eligible veterans and their spouses. **The VA also guarantees loans to purchase mobile homes and plots of land on which to place them.** A veteran who meets any of the following time-in-service criteria is eligible for a VA loan:

- 90 days of active service for veterans of World War II, the Korean War, the Vietnam conflict and the Persian Gulf War.

- A minimum of 181 days of active service during inter-office periods between July 26, 1947 and September 6, 1980.

- Two full years of service during any peacetime period after September 7, 1980.

- Six or more years of continuous duty as a reservist in the Army, Navy, Air Force, Marine Corps or Coast Guard, or as a member of the Army or Air National Guard.

Like the FHA, VA does not loan money. It guarantees loans made by the lending institutions, approved by the agency.

There is no VA dollar limit on the amount of the loan that a veteran can obtain. This is determined by the lender and a qualification of the buyer. However, the VA limits the amount of the loan it will guarantee. As of 2004, the maximum loan now available to a qualified veteran is $ 239,000.00 for a single-family house.

In order to determine what portion of a mortgage loan the VA will guarantee, the veteran must apply for a certificate of eligibility. This certificate does not mean that the veteran will automatically receives a mortgage loan. It merely sets forth the maximum guarantee to which the veteran is entitled. For individuals with full eligibility, no down payment is required for a loan up to the maximum guarantee limit.

Chapter 18

Credit Scores

The loan companies would manually underwrite many of the loans from 10 to 15 years ago but today, **everything is Credit Score driven**. Where do these credit scores come from? Who decides what score we are given? When you apply for a mortgage loan, you will be required to have Credit Scores from the three credit score companies. I call them the "Big 3" –TransUnion, Equifax and Experian. Typically, a credit score can be from 450 - 800. **The higher the score, the better the interest rate and the lower the down payment.** No one has a definite formula for getting a perfect credit score, but we do know a few things about what affects your score.

Your credit score influences everything from the interest rate on your mortgage to the

price you pay for homeowner's insurance premiums. You need to know your credit score from the big three, Experian, Equifax and TransUnion based on information provided by creditors. Scores are based on a formula developed by "Fair Isaac," a research firm. This is important because you need to work on getting the highest score possible since your mortgage interest rate is driven by credit scores. You generally need a score of 620 and above to get a good interest rate.

If your score is below 600, you will be expected to pay above average rate. Those with scores above 720 – 760 rate, usually get the best interest rates. Some of the things that you can do to help your score go up are 1) Earn more money; 2) Pay debts on time; 3) Keep credit card balances below 50% of credit card limit; 4) Do not have a lot of revolving credit; 5) Pay off debt; 6) Pay off large balances; 7) Know that 30, 60, 90 day past due payments will hurt you – pay on time.

Your occupation, age, and employment history do not affect your credit score. Most credit scoring calculations look at the amount of debt you owe compare with your credit limits. **People who have high balances on their credit cards are considered higher risk because they may have trouble making payments.** The formula rewards borrowers who are using credit but using it responsibly. Working on your credit score is very important to getting the best interest rates on your home and investment house. Some mortgage lender will give you "0- down payment investment loan" on a house with a very good interest rate. This means you keep more money in your pocket. It is also good to keep an eye on your credit score to make sure you do not have anything adverse that does not belong there in the first place. You can go to Fair Isaac (www.myfico.com) to get credit scores from the three credit scores companies. However, there is a charge for this.

Chapter 19

Entering Your Promised Land: Have Faith in God

When God's children were trying to enter into their Promised Land, they encountered some obstacles. There were "giants" in the land so to speak. There was also the river Jordan as an obstacle. They had to cross the Jordan to get into the Promised Land. Just like they had to cross the Red Sea on their way out of Egypt and on to the Promised Land, they had to overcome the river Jordan as well. On both occasion, the people murmured in unbelief. **We see here that your obstacles to entering your Promised Land are doubt and unbelief. These are the two biggest giants that normally crop up in our life.**

I want to take you to **Mark 11:22. Jesus said, "Have faith in God." I tell you the truth, if**

anyone says to this mountain, go and throw yourself into to sea and does not doubt in his heart, but believes that what he says will happen, it will be done for him. Therefore I tell you, whatever you ask in prayer, believe that you have received it and it will be yours." So we see here that Jesus is saying, have faith in God. Do not have faith in yourself, but have faith in God.

The problem today is that most people know how to quote scripture. They know the definition of faith but do they understand what they are reading and truly believe in their heart? Maybe this is why we do not see a lot of miracles in the United States as we should.

As mentioned before, my wife and I have traveled to Latin America, South America, Europe, and Africa on mission trips. We plan to go to many other countries. I tell you that the one thing that always moves me is the faith of the people in

Brazil, Ghana, Guatemala and Nigeria. Their faith is so simple but yet so powerful. You can tell they truly believe in their heart what they are saying. We (Americans) may have material possessions but these people from these other countries possess spiritual blessings. The manifestation of the supernatural is an everyday occurrence there but we seldom see the same manifestation of the supernatural here in the US. We need to go after both the spiritual and natural promises of God!

Faith is what it is going to take to be demonstrated the supernatural in the Real Estate Market. Truly, unbelief will be one of the biggest giants you will face in your lifetime. There is always a battle that takes place, as we mentioned earlier in this book, that you would have to go through, especially if it is a blessing from the Lord. I want to tell you that we have seen more non-believers than believers have this kind of faith. What do you mean? I have seen a lot of believers that worry about the down payment; they worry about how they are going to maintain the house, they worry about the interest rate and they worry about getting a good interest rate. They fail to apply their faith and believe God to make a way for them.

Let me tell you something, interest rates are at an all time 40- year low in the mortgage business! I do not know a more opportune time than now to take advantage of this, in the real estate market. Again, I ask you, if not now, when? If not you, who? The devil will come along and fill your mind, with thousands of reasons why you should not think of homeownership. That is where the battle starts, in the mind. **You have got to cut off the voice of the enemy and hear the voice of the true shepherd—the Lord Jesus.**

I go back to this scripture, **"Jesus said, have faith in God."** We also see in the last verse of **Mark 11:25** that the Lord said, **"And when you**

stand praying, if you hold anything against anyone, forgive him so that your Father in heaven may forgive your sins." So, we see **another piece to this puzzle is forgiveness.** You need to forgive people their offences against you if you want to possess your land. We must begin to forgive people, begin to forgive circumstances, and we even have to forgive God for not giving us our inheritance as we want Him to. Maybe it was not the right time; maybe it was not the right place. We must remember that God's time is the best.

As we begin to forgive and confess our sins to God, He cancels them out. **Because it says in 1 John 9, "If we confess our sins, He is faithful and just and will forgive us our sins and purify us from all unrighteousness."** God will prosper you. **Proverbs 28:13 says, "He who conceals his sin does not prosper, but he who confesses his sin does prosper."** I want to add that many Christians do not know how to confess sins to one another and that they ignore their sins. We are also commanded to confess ours sins to one another. God is giving us this simple solution to confess our sin to one another so that we may be healed. Unconfessed sins allow the devil to operate in our lives so that God cannot prosper us.

Chapter 20

The Hall of Faith

This is what the word says **the definition of faith is, (Hebrews 11:1) "Now faith is being sure of what we hope for and certain of what we do not see."** This is a very important verse that I believe pertains to real estate. These are things that we do not see and that we must see with the eye of faith—the eyes of our heart! We have to believe that we are going to possess our Promised Land. We have to believe that it is our inheritance and that it is God's promise to us . **Please take time to meditate on this.**

God said to Joshua (Joshua 1:8), to meditate day and night upon His word and he would be successful and he would be prosperous. We therefore must be like Joshua and meditate because this is what it is going to take to get real estate. It says in **Hebrews 11: 6** says, **"without faith it is impossible to please God because anyone who comes to Him, must believe that He exists and that he rewards those who earnestly seek Him."** If you are earnestly seeking God, your faith will be build up and it will increase. We see that it is recorded in Verse 8 that, **"By faith, Abraham, when called to go to a place he would later receive as an inheritance, obeyed and went, even though he did not know where he was going."** We see here that Abraham did not know where he was going, yet God told him to "go to a land which I am giving you." He went by faith, not seeing that land with his physical eyes but I believe that he saw it with his heart and he believed God. In demonstration of his great faith, he got up, packed up and went.

This is the same kind of faith that will take you out of an apartment complex, this is the same kind of faith that will take you out of the

projects, this is the same kind of faith that will take you out of the place you are right now and into the place of destiny, into the place of promise and into the place of inheritance. This kind of faith will take you to the next level, and will take you to the place where you are destined.

I want to share a story with you that recently happened while writing this book. We were working with a pastor who came to me and said, "Edward, we need to find a commercial space approximately so many square feet and we need to find it today." Sometimes, these pastors from other countries do not understand how the United States works when it comes to real estate. But I had faith and he had faith, so I went to work to find him a space. We had put an application in with one company. I called time and time again without any response back from the company. After three or four days, I said, I am going to look for another place because they are not responding to us. I told him that did not believe that the property was the one that God wanted for him. I have learned by experience to move on when people do not respond. I just find someone else who will respond.

Normally God is closing one door and opening another door at the same time. He needed the place within a certain amount of time and he needed to get into it quickly. I told him that he basically needed a miracle, with the financing and everything else. It was about 4:00 pm one evening and we were looking at the last property. We called the number on the billboard on the property and asked, "Where is this suite for rent, we can't find it?" We later discovered that a trailer truck was blocking the Leasing Space and that was why we could not see it. The owner/realtor said, "It's around the corner, right here." So, we went in. We looked around and it was what he needed. We were quiet, and the realtor went on to say, "You can have this place (it was approximately 960 to 1000 square feet), **"as is,"** for one year and for $1000 a month!" This is a commercial property alongside a very major road in Atlanta, Georgia. I was sitting there thinking, "This is God, it's 4:30 in the afternoon, and the Pastor needs a place today. This guy is giving this to him, **"as is,"** and he is willing to do a one-year lease!

Usually, commercial property owners want a three to five year lease. That was one thing that really amazed me. The second thing I said to the gentleman is, "O.K, give me a minute with the pastor." I spoke to the pastor and said, "Do you want this?" He said, "Yes, I'll take this." I told him that I did not want him to let the realtor know just how desperate his was to get the space. I have a policy of not letting realtors know when my clients are desperate. I usually tell them to remain calm until after the deal is signed. So I said to the owner, "O.K., we'll take this place." He said, "Do you want to sign the agreement, right now? If you are, this is what I'll need, one months rent and one months deposit." I said, "O.K., that's not bad." I said, "We'll come back to tomorrow and sign the agreement and we'll get a cashier's check for one month's rent which is also the one month's deposit" and we left. **The extraordinary thing was that we never filled out any paperwork for a credit check or background check.** I told this pastor, "This is phenomenal! I have never seen this on a commercial piece of property. This is a miracle. This must be the place that God has for you!"

We came back early the next morning and we signed the agreement. He paid his money and got a copy of the lease and off we went. The pastor had the place that he desired. The realtor said to me, "This is the fastest transaction I've ever signed an agreement on to give out a commercial space." I said, "We work fast, we have faith in God." We shook hands before we left.

I want to tell you something, if God can do that for this man, He can do it for you. He is not special just because he is a pastor. He had faith to know that we could find a place and that God would direct us. We did not know where God wanted us to go and look for the property but we believed in our hearts for God to send a miracle to help this pastor.

Again, I want to tell you that God can perform that same miracle that he performed for the pastor. He can perform it for you! **God has no favorites. God wants to perform the same type of miracle for you.** God wants to put you into a place where you can prosper. Miracles do happen today for those who have faith in God. If you believe in your heart as the word says, God will give this to you.

Hebrews 11:32 says, "What more shall I say, I do not have time to tell you about Gideon,

Barrick, Samson, Jehosaphat, David, Samuel and the prophets who through faith conquered kingdoms, administered justice, gained what was promised, who shut the mouths of lions, quenched the fury of the flames, who escaped the edge of the sword, whose weakness was turned to strength, who became powerful in battle and routed foreign armies. Women received back their dead, raised to life again." Beloved, I want to tell you. **That same resurrection power can work for your house, it can work for your investment property and it can work in all areas of your life**, if you believe what God's word says. If you get it in your heart and you begin to walk it out like Joshua, you will experience God's miracles. We are told in **Joshua 1:3** that wherever he put his foot, God gave him the land to possess.

Chapter 21

Strategy:
Get God's Strategy to Possess
Your Inheritance

We need to ask God for wisdom. We need
to begin to pray for direction. We need to believe
and pray for the opportunity to come about for us to
possess our inheritance. We know that God has
promised us this inheritance. We must remind God
of His promises. **Isaiah 55:11 says, "It is my
word that goes out from my mouth, it will not
return to me empty but it will accomplish what I
desire and achieve the purpose for which I have
sent it."** We see that God's word does not return
void but it accomplishes what it is sent to do. This
is one of my favorite scriptures that I have declared
many times and still declare over my life and I
believe it with my whole heart.

I believe that if God says it, it must be true. Like Joshua and Caleb, if God said that he has given us the land and we are to possess it, it must be true. We have to begin to get that kind of spirit within us, that conquering, warrior type spirit. God has said, this is ours and there is an intruder, the devil and his spirits. **There are intruders and squatters on our land and they have been occupying our land long enough. It is now time to drive them out.** Now is time to go into our land because God says, "I've given you this land. I've given you this inheritance; I've given you this promise."

He said to that to Joshua and "the gang" so to speak. 1) They had to go and do something; 2) they had to go over; 3) they had to go and possess the land. We know that with Joshua, every battle was different. He had to hear the word of the Lord for success in each battle. I am not going to sit here and tell you that every real estate transaction is the same. It is not. One of the reasons I am in real estate is because it is so challenging; it is so different. Every case is different; every opportunity brings a different crisis. My wife and I get paid to solve problems. That is, we are paid to resolve people's issues concerning buying and selling a home. You will have to hear God on how to solve your problems; you will have to figure it out. I do not know anybody who has this "down pack." There is always something new that we are learning in real estate. I would just remind you again to really learn to hear the voice of the Lord and what He has promised you. **Believe it, go out and begin to slay those giants in your life. Begin to possess what is rightfully yours.**

Chapter 22

Receiving Your Double Portion

We see here, in **Proverbs 22:7** that, **"the borrower is a slave to the lender."** Ask God to erase the debt. Ask God to help you make more money and to work smarter and not harder. Believe in God to make you a landowner. It is His will to give you not just one house but two houses and much more if you believe. You ask, Edward, "I can barely get one, what do you mean two?" Once again, I believe God's word and I believe that God has given us the revelation in **Isaiah 61:7.** It says, **"Instead of their shame, my people will receive a double portion, instead of disgrace, they will rejoice in their inheritance." So they will inherit a double portion in their land.** God wants to give you double, my beloved, double!

Do you remember in 2 Kings 2:9 when Elisha was with Elijah and he asked for the double portion because he knew that the single portion would not be enough for him. He needed that double portion. **This is another key that I want to give you. Pray for the double portion of God to be in your life, that you want double of everything.** You do not want just one but two of everything God has for you. You want two houses, you want two cars and you want two businesses. You want that double portion. Begin to believe that and you will see God move on your behalf.

There was a time in my life that God had told me about receiving the double portion in my life. I am not into numerology, but I remember one year that everywhere I went I saw the number two. I would look at the clock at night and it would be 2:22. I would be driving in my car and it would be 2:22 in the afternoon. I would look at my watch and it would be 2:22. God began to speak to me because I was confessing, I believed God God's Word and I was getting the Word into my heart that I needed the double portion in my life. To defeat the giants in my life, I had to get into God's promises for me and take hold of them. You can do the same thing too! After my wife prophesied, we began to look for property in the area that we wanted to live. We prayed that God would help us find a good deal on a house. We did find a great deal on the house that we live in currently because we declared and believed that what God said was true. We are always asking God to give us great deals. We are not special, we just believe and if you start to ask God to do the same for you, He will begin to bring you those great deals in business too.

Finally, you need to begin to look for an area in which you would like to live and start prophesying that your home is in the area. Start prophesying that God is going to give you a home there; that God will give it to you and start believing it and start looking for that opportunity. I believe that as you begin to look and work with what you have, God will begin to open doors for you. You will walk into your inheritance.

I want to share one more scripture with you. **I Chronicles 28:8, "Be careful to follow all the commands of the Lord your God that you may possess this good land and pass it on as an inheritance to your descendents, forever."** We see here that one of the other reasons God gives you land, gives you the double inheritance in land, is so that you can pass this on to your descendents, that you could give them something. It is much better for you to give it to your family than for your family to have to struggle and struggle to obtain some land. This is why God ultimately wants to give you that double portion.

Chapter 23

The Landowners and the Homeowners

We see here in **Acts 4:34** that, **"There were no needy persons among them. From time to time, those who owned land or houses, sold them, brought the money from the sales and put it at the apostle's feet. It was distributed to anyone as he had need."** We see here another reason that God may put it upon your heart to be a landowner, to own several pieces of land, to own several houses and to own several investment properties. I believe that from time to time, God might say, "O.K. son or O.K. daughter, when I tell you to sell that house, when I tell you to sell that land, you're going to take a percentage of that and you're going to give it away or you may give all the money that you make from that away."

The Lord showed me a revelation that the above scripture is to help us understand why He wants us to be landowners. It is not just so that we can have it for ourselves but I it is so that we can give to others. Do you know that my wife and I have for several years dreamed of being able to house pastors? A strong dream in our hearts has been to take care of ministries. That is a very good dream, I believe. We believe that God would bring all these pastors and ministries our way and that we would connect with. If they do not have a house, we pray that we would help them get from an apartment into a nice house. I want to encourage you in this. Beloved, we are currently doing this. God hears prayers and He is doing it through us.

This is a great thing to do for God, to get land, to get investment property, to get rental property and be able to share it with others and be able to help God's ministers get into a home. You know that they are working for the Lord; they are bringing souls into the kingdom. They are advancing the kingdom. They are working directly for God. They may not have a lot of money but they are God's representatives and God wants to take care of them. If you take care of them, He will take care of you. If you take care of God's people, He will take care of you. He will make sure that everything is O.K. This is just a great vision and idea to take hold of and I hope you will.

I would like to inspire many people who have a heart for God to get wealth, to do this. Honor God with your wealth and honor God with your ownership and in return, God will honor you. The true ownership of all things belong to God because He owns everything including, **"the cattle on a thousand hills." He owns the earth and the fullness thereof (Psalms 50: 10-12).** God is looking and waiting to bestow His blessing upon His servants who have a right heart, a right attitude, and a right mind to think of the will of God and to go out and possess the land. **Believe me, there is nothing like home ownership.**

Chapter 24

Nothing Like Homeownership

I remember the reason we got into this business was because my wife had bought her house on the north side of Atlanta and the agent was supposed to have them do certain things to the house and when she moved into the house they had not done anything! They did not replace the carpet and they did not even paint the house as they promised. We went back to the real estate agent. He told us it was too late and we had already closed on the house. He just gave us excuse after excuse. He finally gave us a couple of hundred dollars but we ended up putting about two to three thousand dollars into fixing up this house. It was really frustrating.

I was sitting one day watching public television after I had prayed that week saying,

"Lord, what can I do with my skills to best help people and to make income?" The Lord spoke to me saying, "Get into real estate." That week, we saw a documentary on real estate on television. We learned that it was going to be on the upper swing for the next 5 to 7 years. We decided to get into real estate. I want to encourage you by telling you that we are now on our fourth year as real estate agents. If God can do it with two people who had no knowledge of real estate, had no background in real estate, He can do it with you. We just had a desire and a passion and a hunger to see this work. Let me tell you, we get clients all the time, from different income levels and backgrounds that say, "I'm glad you told us about ownership." I'm glad you encouraged us to get a home because there is no other feeling like being a homeowner."

When you get out of your apartment, you will be fortunate to get your deposit back plus the manager might be upset because they lost a

tenant. When you sell a house after living in it for about two to five years, you should make several thousands of dollars if not tens of thousands of dollars. If the appreciation has been going at an average national rate, you should make money on the house and that will make you feel good. You can take some of that money that you got when you sold your house and you buy another one. You can even buy two houses and live in and rent the other. This is what I feel is your inheritance and the will of God. I want to pray for you now. I pray in the name of Jesus that God may anoint you as the priests of your home, to go and get land. That God would put his hand upon you, that He would bless you and that He would enlarge your territory and enlarge your vision. **That He would enlarge your heart for vision, that He would enlarge your influence and that He would enlarge your bank accounts.** That He would begin to move upon you with vision and with clarity and with focus so and that you can see that you are a titled landowner by

God and that you have an inheritance that is rightfully yours. That you would rise up with boldness as we read in Hebrews and begin to possess the land that God has for you.

Chapter 25

An Investor's First Time at Investment Property

My wife had a friend that she knows from a Brazilian church in Marietta, Georgia. He wanted to buy his first investment property—to buy, fix and sell. We had found a property where he had to put up $5,000.00 to purchase. On the day of closing, we were told that a church wanted to buy the property immediately. We were in awe of how quick God was at work. The church made an offer to buy the property within 30 days and paid cash. My wife's friend made $10,000.00 and never made one payment on the house or did any repairs. **He does not even speak good English.** He just trusted us to help him find a property that he could make some money on. We wrote the contract the next day after he bought the house. **I always say that God is the best business partner and He does**

expect a return on his investment. If you do not believe that, then read the parable about the two talents in **Luke 19:23**.

Chapter 26

Praying in Faith

I would again like to pray for you for a moment. Begin to meditate on these words, let them saturate your heart. "Father, I pray in the name of Jesus for the spirit of Elijah, that landowner anointing, to come upon those who read this book. I pray Father God that you would anoint them to possess the land, to possess the inheritance that you have given them and that they would be landowners and homeowners. I pray that they would be a blessing to the nations, Lord (Proverbs 13:22). I also pray that they would get the wealth of the wicked that is stored up for them in Christ Jesus. Father, you said in Deuteronomy 8:18, that you give us the power and the ability for wealth, Lord. That is a covenant you gave to Abraham, Isaac and Jacob and You swore by that covenant to his sees also.

You said that whatever our hands do shall prosper and that Your desire that we prosper in our soul, our body, our mind, our spirit, our heart and our businesses. It is Your will for us to enlarge our real estate territory and to give us abundant favor and grace, as we have never experience before in our lives. I pray that Lord, God, that You would begin to fight and destroy our enemies. You want to see everything we do turn to gold, Lord. Father, I pray that you would give to all those that read this book, a spirit of creativity. Let them have creativity in their finances and also let then have the creativity that will open doors for them. Lord, stir them up to look for land, stir them up to look for apartments, stir them up to look for strip malls, stir them up to look for huge towers of property and to go and possess the land. Father, I pray that you would bless them in Jesus mighty name and that they will get their rightful inheritance from you, now, while they are alive. In Jesus Mighty name!

Charts

Note: *All Charts in this book are used by permission from Real Net USA.*

Commentary: These charts come from an investment company that several of our investors and I have purchased wholesale property from. My question to you is where can you invest little of your money and make appreciation on the entire investment? In other words, lets say you invest $5000.00 dollars in a C.D or money market account or IRA or anything else for that matter but you only get paid on the money you invested— the $5000.00. But in real estate, it is different. Let me explain; if you invested $5000.00 on a property that was worth $100,000.00, you would make an average of 6-8% appreciation on the total value of the house and not just the $5000.00 you invested. So, I believe that real estate is a much better investment. Remember that land generally does not decrease in price but always goes up.

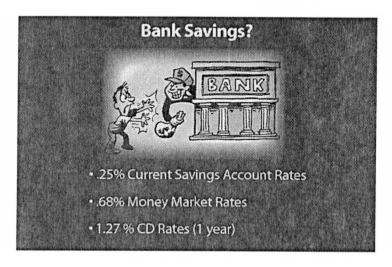

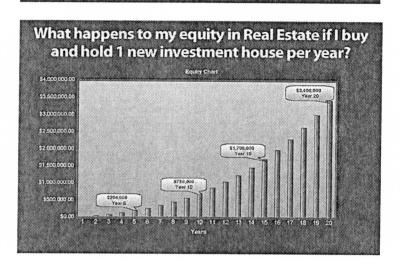

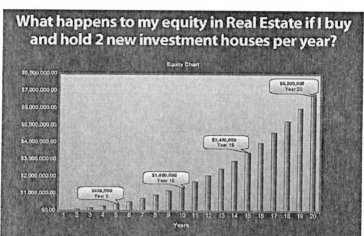

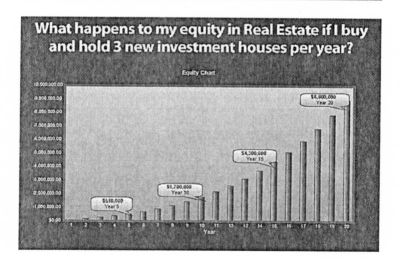

How did all these people make millions in real estate?

Simple Principles:

1 **O.P.M.-** Use Other People's Money to leverage your own investment capital.

2 **Never Sell-** Hold the real estate investments long term.

3 **Run a Tight Ship-** Treat investing like a business, get good at it and run it efficiently.

4 **Be Consistent and Persistent-** Repeat steps 1, 2, and 3 above over and over again.

The secret to real estate wealth building can be summarized by this simple equation:

$$A + A = E$$

(Appreciation) (Amortization) (Equity)

Real estate wealth building occurs when Appreciation and Amortization is applied to a large pool of rental properties that are accumulated by running **1** through **4** above consistently.

Why Doesn't Everyone Try to Build Wealth with Real Estate Investment?

Barriers to entry into the real estate investment business

- Don't understand the basic principles of real estate investing: $A + A = E$;

- Don't have good enough credit to access O.P.M. (other people's money);

- Don't know how or where to find investment opportunities at wholesale prices;

- Don't know how to access O.P.M. to finance the investment properties;

- Don't know how to manage rehab or property rental;

You need a MENTOR to provide encouragement, confidence, and show you how to get started.

EJM Enterprises

EJM Enterprise Product Order Form

No.	Item Description	Price Ea	Quantity	Total
01	Investment Property – CD's with Book	$150.00		
02	Investment Property – Tapes with Book	$150.00		
03	Evangelism Manual for Teaching Classes	$10.00		
04	Basic Principles of Possessing the Land - CD	$12.00		
05	Basic Principles of Possessing the Land – Tape	$10.00		
06	Evangelism In Today's Marketplace – CD	$10.00		
07	Evangelism In Today's Marketplace – Tape	$9.00		
08	Aromatherapy CD Set	$15.00		
09	Aromatherapy Tape Set	$10.00		
10	A Double Portion by Yaw Owusu-Achaw - CD	$12.00		
11	*King of Kings Anointing Oil-2- 4once bottles	$35.00		
12	Possessing the Land - Book	$12.95		

* = Includes FREE Display Kit

	Total	

(In USA) Shipping & handling for Book, CD's, Tapes & Manual is $5.00

COPY OR CUT OUT THIS
ORDER FORM & COUPON
FOR AN INSTANT
MAIL-IN DISCOUNT ON
"INVESTMENT PROPERTY"
CD OR TAPE
WITH MANUAL TODAY!

SAVE $25.00

FREE SHIPPING in USA
with coupon!

Please ship my order to the following address.

Name:_____ Date: _____

Address:_____

City:_____ State:_____ Zip:_____

Phone:_____ e-mail address:_____

Mail completed Order Form to:
EJM Enterprises
Attn: Edward Murray
651 Exchange Place
Lilburn, GA 30047

ejmenterprise@bellsouth.net

157

Shipping and handling for Anointing Oil,
tapes & CD's $5.00
Investment Property with Manual is $10.00

A Division of EJM Enterprises

Investment Property

This course teaches everything you need to know to get you
started on investment properties

Foreclosures
Renovating Property
Conventional, VA & FHA
Hard Money Lenders
Contracts & Credit Scores
Rental Applications & Agreements

A Division of EJM Enterprises

Basic Principles of Possessing the Land

Real Estate for the Market Place
Real Estate based on Biblical Principles

Soaring with Eagles Ministries

A Division of EJM Enterprises

Aromatherapy

Edward Murray C.M.T.

This 2 tape series is an informative teaching on aromatherapy
This seminar is about the following:

- Usage and Application of the Essential Oils
- Learn over 12 Essential Oils and Their Usage
- Blending of Essential Oils for Disease
- Contraindications to Aromatherapy

- Aromatherapy Massage Techniques
- The Theory of Essential Oils
- History of Aromatherapy
- Cost of Essential Oils
- Blend for Hair Loss
- Safety Precautions
- Blend for Stress

A Division of EJM Enterprises

Evangelism In Today's Marketplace

How to share the word of God in the Marketplace
How to share God's Heart with the lost anywhere,
anytime or any place

A Division of EJM Enterprises

A Double Portion by Yaw Owusu-Achaw

The Greatest need for the hour is God's Power working in our lives

Satan's people are manifesting two times Satan's personalities on the planet

We already have the victory, we as God's people need to learn to walk in it and trust God as Elisha did

162

TO HIS GLORY PUBLISHING COMPANY, INC.

111 Sunnydale Court, Lawrenceville, GA 30044,   U.S.A.

Order Form for Bookstores

Order Date: _____

Order Placed B _____

Address: _____

City_____ ST/ZIP_____

Phone#:_____

Email:_____

Purchase Order#:_____

By fax:

By phone:
Terms:

Discount:
Return Policy: Within 1 Year

Title and ISBN#	Quantity	List Price
Shipping Method:		
Media		
UPS		
FedEx		
Other (please describe)		

Ship To Address:

_____
_____
_____
_____
_____
_____

Bill To Address:

_____
_____
_____
_____
_____
_____

TO HIS GLORY PUBLISHING COMPANY, INC Use Only - Billing Information

Invoice No.:_____   Invoice Amount:_____   Invoice Date:_____

Printed in the United States
25529LVS00001B/205-210

9 780974 980232